ISSUES IN SPORTS

VIOLENCE

IN SPORTS

BY PAUL BOWKER

Published by ABDO Publishing Company, PO Box 398166, Minneapolis, MN 55439. Copyright © 2014 by Abdo Consulting Group, Inc. International copyrights reserved in all countries. No part of this book may be reproduced in any form without written permission from the publisher. SportsZone™ is a trademark and logo of ABDO Publishing Company.

Printed in the United States of America,
North Mankato, Minnesota
102013
012014

Editor: Chrös McDougall
Series Designer: Craig Hinton

Photo credits: Katerina Sulova/CTK/AP Images, cover, 1; Duane Burleson/AP Images, 5, 6; Noah Berger/AP Images, 10, 13; San Francisco Giants, HO/AP Images, 15; Kelley L. Cox/Icon SMI, 18; Charles Krupa/AP Images, 21; Kostas Lymperopoulos/Cal Sport Media via AP Images, 23; Charlie Neibergall/AP Images, 25; Mary Ann Chastain/AP Images, 27; Mel Evans/AP Images, 29; Chris Volpe/New Haven Register/AP Images, 31; Will Vragovic/The Tampa Bay Times/AP Images, 34; imago sportfotodienst/ActionPlus/Corbis, 39; AP Images, 41; Press Association via AP Images, 42; Andres Kudacki/AP Images, 45; Action Plus Sports Images/Corbis, 46; Gregorio Borgia/AP Images, 49; Amanda Sowards/Montgomery Advertiser/AP Images, 51; Daniel Brenner/AnnArbor.com/AP Images, 53; Ted S. Warren/AP Images, 55; Matt Rourke/AP Images, 59

Library of Congress Control Number: 2013946585

Cataloging-in-Publication Data

Bowker, Paul, 1954-
 Violence in sports / Paul Bowker.
   p. cm. -- (Issues in sports)
Includes bibliographical references and index.
ISBN 978-1-62403-125-0
1. Violence in sports--Juvenile literature.   I. Title.
796--dc23

                                        2013946585

Content Consultant: Alex B. Diamond, D.O., M.P.H.
Assistant Professor of Orthopaedics and Rehabilitation
Assistant Professor of Pediatrics
Medical Director, Program for Injury Prevention in Youth Sports (PIPYS)
Vanderbilt University Medical Center
Team Physician - Vanderbilt University, Nashville Predators, Nashville Sounds
Vanderbilt Sports Medicine

TABLE OF CONTENTS

MAY 0 6 2014

Indiana Pacers forward Ron Artest is restrained by a teammate during the brawl that took place in the 2004 NBA game against the Detroit Pistons.

UGLY BEHAVIOR

The Indiana Pacers led the Detroit Pistons 97–82 late in a 2004 National Basketball Association (NBA) game. With approximately 46 seconds left in the game, Pistons center Ben Wallace went for a layup. As he did, Pacers forward Ron Artest shoved him from behind. It was a hard foul, but the play was not all that unusual.

Still, the foul made the Pistons players angry. The home fans at the Palace of Auburn Hills in Michigan booed Artest. Then Wallace shoved Artest hard. At first the other players tried to hold Artest and Wallace apart. Then players from each team began to push and shove each other. Before long the benches had cleared. Coaches stepped in to try to break

▲ The Pacers' Ron Artest wrestles with fans during the 2004 fight at the Palace of Auburn Hills.

them up. Tensions had heated up in a matter of seconds. But at this point it was still merely a shoving match between the NBA players.

Artest tried to escape the melee by lying down on the scorers' table. Soon the scuffle on the court appeared to be winding down. Then a fan threw a drink cup that landed on Artest's chest. That is when things turned ugly.

Artest shot up and charged into the stands. He went straight for a fan sitting a few rows up. Artest thought that fan had thrown the cup and began punching him. Other players joined Artest in the stands. Some players tried to pull him out. Others joined in the fight as fans and players threw punches at each other. At one point a chair was tossed.

The players finally made their way back to the court. Then some other fans came onto the court to taunt the Pacers. Artest and teammate Stephen Jackson responded by punching some of them.

Officials declared the game over. The Pacers had won. Now the players just had to get off the court. But the Pistons fans were livid. Pacers players had to cover their heads as they made for the tunnel leading to the locker room. Fans in the stands above the tunnel threw bottles, cups, and other debris at the players.

"I just remember standing at half-court and being kind of helpless," Pistons coach Larry Brown said. "I did try to get to the microphone [to tell the fans to calm down], but there was so much going on and there were so many things on my mind. I just felt sick to my stomach to see what transpired."

NATIONAL DISCUSSION

The 2004 Pacers-Pistons game was broadcast nationally on ESPN. Thousands of fans watched live as an ordinary basketball game turned into one of the worst brawls between fans and players in US sports history. Highlights and analysis of the "Malice in the Palace," which the incident came to be called, continued throughout the night.

Some pundits blamed Wallace for the brawl. They believed he overreacted to the initial foul. Others blamed Artest. They said he and his teammates should have had better self-control and stayed out of the stands. Many people, however, blamed the fans. It is never acceptable to throw anything at players or to come onto the court, they said.

Several involved parties were punished. Criminal assault charges were filed against five players and also against five spectators. Two more fans were charged with trespassing on the court. The Auburn Hills, Michigan, police produced a report of nearly 900 pages. The NBA ended up suspending nine players from both teams. The steepest penalty went to Artest. He was suspended for the remaining 73 games that season plus the playoffs. In total he lost nearly $5 million in salary from the suspension.

The incident was a black eye for the entire league. It also began a wider national discussion about fan violence at sporting events. Few incidents have been as visible as the Malice in the Palace. But violence at sporting events or among sports fans was not new.

HISTORY OF SCUFFLES

NBA fights are not new. Paul Silas was a professional basketball player for 16 years before he turned to coaching. He remembers a game in 1968 between the Atlanta Hawks and the New York Knicks. Several players got into a scuffle. Fighting also broke out in the stands. Silas got into a fight with Phil Jackson, who played for the Knicks. Lou Hudson punched Knicks center Willis Reed. Silas recalled that Knicks player Nate Bowman and Hawks player Bill Bridges were wrestling in the stands. Bowman took a "merciless pounding" from Hawks fans. "That was just one of 'em," Silas said.

FAN VIOLENCE

In major professional sports, players often scuffle during the games, but violence is more common among fans. Sometimes it is as simple as throwing things at each other. But in extreme cases, fans have been beaten up or even stabbed outside of stadiums.

There are several reasons fans might fight. By nature, most sports position two parties directly against each other. In addition, many sports fans are very passionate. These two factors can lead to conflicts. Fans might disagree over a call or a rough play. Or in some cases, people simply do not like other people who support a different athlete or team.

In the United States, most sports teams simply represent a city or a school. In other countries, sports teams sometimes represent much more. In Scotland, the two biggest teams both play in Glasgow. Celtic and Rangers have been rivals for more than a century, and their conflicts sometimes go beyond the score in soccer games. Celtic fans traditionally are Irish Catholics who support an independent Scotland. Meanwhile, Rangers fans are traditionally Protestants who support Scotland being in the United Kingdom. These sorts of deep, emotional connections are common among soccer teams and their fans.

Alcohol is often another contributing factor in fan violence. Some people like to drink a lot of alcohol at or before sporting events. This impairs their judgment. Sometimes they act in ways that they normally would not. Experts say that alcohol and other drugs are at the heart of most fan violence.

RIOTS AND CELEBRATIONS

Sporting events tend to stir up people's emotions. At the end of a big game, fans have been known to let loose. Sometimes they let loose in celebration. In college sports, fans sometimes storm the basketball court or football field after a big win. On the surface this appears to be a harmless celebration. However, this action puts players at risk of being attacked. Even fans are vulnerable of being trampled by other rushing fans. One tradition at football games is for fans to pull down the goalposts after an important victory. But people have been seriously hurt and have even died when the goalposts come crashing down.

In 2012, the San Francisco Giants beat the Detroit Tigers to win the World Series. The celebration on the streets of San Francisco soon grew out of control. A public transit bus was set on fire, as were other things. Police showed up in riot gear to handle the crowds. The police also escorted firefighters to put out the fires. This was not the first time a World Series win led to such behavior. In 1984, a police car was overturned and set on fire following the Tigers' World Series win. One person died and 80 were injured during that riot.

Yet at other times, fans let loose in destructive ways after a defeat. Vancouver Canucks hockey fans rioted after their team lost in the 2011 Stanley Cup. They turned over cars, started fires, and smashed shop windows in downtown Vancouver.

NOT JUST MAJOR SPORTS

Violent events at major professional or college sporting events tend to get the most attention. Violence is hardly limited to these big-time events, though.

Even youth sports are at risk. In January 2013, a student from Morgan Park High School in Chicago was shot and killed in a parking lot after a basketball game. That game had even been played at a neutral location to try to limit the tensions between the rival fans. Smaller altercations between fans from rival schools take place after games across the nation every year. Sometimes the violence spreads further. Youth soccer officials and baseball umpires have been assaulted. In 2013, a youth soccer official

CULTURE OF HOCKEY

Fights in professional hockey games are common. For many fans, fighting is an important part of the game. They say it polices the game. That means a player might be less likely to hit an opponent if the hit might lead to a fight. To some fans, however, hockey fights are just part of the entertainment. Several Web sites have produced lists of the top 10 hockey fights of all time. Hockeyfights.com has a fight log to track hockey fights.

Fighting has become a part of the hockey culture, and sometimes those fights spread into the stands. In a March 2001 National Hockey League (NHL) game, Tie Domi of the Toronto Maple Leafs was sent to the penalty box. But some Philadelphia Flyers fans were throwing things at him. First Domi squirted water at the fans. Eventually one fan tumbled into the penalty box with Domi and the two began wrestling.

"They threw stuff at me," Domi said. "Once was enough. After the second one, I told the guy in the penalty box that after one more I was going to squirt water. So I squirted water. I didn't plan on fighting anybody."

in Utah died as the result of a physical assault. Parents sometimes get into fights in the stands.

Sports are becoming more and more popular in the United States and around the world. Participation in youth sports is booming. Professional athletes are being paid more than ever. And sporting events and news about sports are big businesses. As attention to sports grows, sports leagues, school administrators, parents, and even governments are stepping up to try to eliminate violence. They hope to understand why sports sometimes provoke violence and how they can stop it.

AFTERMATH OF THE MALICE IN THE PALACE

In the case of the Pacers-Pistons brawl, NBA Commissioner David Stern blamed the event on "15 fans and five players."

Rick Carlisle was the Pacers' coach at the time of the brawl. He blamed the Pistons for having poor security. He also said the

team should have gotten Ben Wallace off the court quickly. It was Wallace
who shoved Ron Artest following the foul. That led to more pushing
and shoving.

Stern reacted to the brawl by suspending Artest for the rest of the
season. He also suspended Stephen Jackson of the Pacers for 30 games
and Jermaine O'Neal of the Pacers for 15 games.

The 2004 NBA game drove home a strong point: Violence can quickly
surface at an athletic contest. To prevent such violence—or minimize it—
teams, athletes, fans, security forces, and police must be better prepared.

CHAPTER 2

A film strip shows a famous 1965 fight between the San Francisco Giants' Juan Marichal (27) and the Los Angeles Dodgers' John Roseboro, left. ▶

THE HEATED RIVALRIES

Sports rivalries intensify emotions in fans. This happens at all levels of sports, from high school to college to professional sports. Sometimes it is just because teams play each other often and develop an intense desire to beat each other. Other times it is simply because the opponent represents a different city, school, or culture. Either way, sports rivalries are often at the heart of fan violence.

There are many storied rivalries in US professional sports. Fans from around the country tune in when the Boston Red Sox play the New York Yankees in baseball. However, the rivalry between the Los Angeles Dodgers and San Francisco Giants goes a bit deeper.

Both teams are among the oldest in baseball. And both teams originated in New York City. The New York Giants played in Manhattan, while the Dodgers played just across the East River in Brooklyn. The fans mostly changed in 1958 when both teams moved to California. But the regional bragging rights remained.

The Dodgers and Giants were baseball's only West Coast teams at the time. The closest team to the east was in Kansas City. The Dodgers and Giants represented the two most famous cities on the West Coast. They were always trying to prove theirs was the better city. Now they could do that through baseball, too.

Major League Baseball (MLB) has expanded since then. Now there are five teams in California. Still, the rivalry between the Dodgers and Giants remains intense. In 2010, the Giants earned bragging rights by winning the World Series. A Giants fan named Bryan Stow traveled with some friends to Los Angeles to watch 2011 Opening Day against the Dodgers.

Stow wore Giants colors to the game. Afterward, some Dodgers fans confronted him in the parking lot. The Dodgers fans brutally beat him. They left him unconscious on the ground. Stow survived, but he suffered a traumatic brain injury and was permanently disabled.

The incident put a spotlight on stadium security. The team and local police tried to assure fans that baseball games were safe.

"It's not necessarily baseball fans [who cause trouble]," Los Angeles Police Department deputy chief Jose Perez said before Opening Day 2012.

"You have a couple of knuckleheads who for some reason commit criminal acts."

Still, the incident showed what could happen when fans get upset. Several different parties scrambled to improve fan safety. Security at Dodger Stadium was increased. However, the Stow family filed suit against the team. The suit claimed that previous security cutbacks were responsible for the attack.

The attack also prompted some independent people to take action. A group of California-based fans started a Web site called fansagainstviolence.com. The site focuses on raising awareness of safety at stadiums. The National Football League's (NFL's) Oakland Raiders were among the teams working in partnership with fansagainstviolence.com. The team even created a fans' code of conduct. Mike Gatto, a state representative from Los Angeles, authored a bill. The Improving Personal Safety at Stadiums Act passed in 2012. It required major professional sports teams to clearly post the phone numbers at which fans could reach security.

TAKING A STAND

"Many parents have told me that they are afraid to take their kids to a ballgame. This law will allow fans to report incidents to stadium security before they escalate out of control. . . . It has become apparent that we need to act to keep the action at professional games on the field and out of the stands. AB 2464 is a simple, common-sense, and preventative solution."

—California Assemblyman Mike Gatto on his 2012 bill that requires major-league sports stadiums in California to post telephone numbers or text-messaging codes that fans can use immediately in case of trouble

Los Angeles Dodgers and San Francisco Giants players stand together to condemn fan violence after the Brian Stow incident in April 2011.

OTHER ATTACKS

The Stow beating was particularly violent. However, rivalry-motivated fights are common at sports stadiums and arenas around the world.

The Oakland Raiders are known for having some of the most intense fans of any team in the United States. One of the Raiders' biggest rivals is the San Francisco 49ers. The teams play just a few miles apart. In 2011, two men were shot in the parking lot and one man was severely beaten in a restroom during a game between those teams.

In 2010, fans clashed before the annual University of Southern California (USC) vs. University of California, Los Angeles (UCLA) football game. Some fans showed up at the Rose Bowl in Pasadena, California, several hours before the game to tailgate. That afternoon, a fight broke out. Police said approximately 40 people were involved. One man was stabbed and three were arrested. It took police 15 minutes to break up the fight.

Fights can be commonplace in and around stadiums on game days. But fights also happen away from the playing field.

Boston Red Sox and New York Yankees fans love to argue about their teams. In October 2010, two men were doing just that at a restaurant in Branford, Connecticut. But the argument escalated. Eventually the Yankees fan stabbed the Red Sox fan in the neck. He was arrested soon afterward.

In college basketball, few fans are more intense than those in Kentucky. In March 2012, a 71-year-old University of Louisville fan punched a 68-year-old University of Kentucky fan at a dialysis clinic in Georgetown, Kentucky. They were arguing over basketball. Kentucky and Louisville are college basketball rivals.

A Chicago White Sox baseball fan was blinded as a result of an argument with a Chicago Cubs fan. The incident happened at a family birthday party in July 2008. Cubs fans and brothers Bob and Jerry Czapla attacked Jerry's brother-in-law Robert Steele, a White Sox fan. Bob was sentenced to three years in jail for the attack. Jerry was sentenced to six months in jail.

UNITED IN BOSTON

Perhaps no rivalry in US professional sports is as heated as that between the Boston Red Sox and the New York Yankees. But those hard feelings were put aside briefly in 2013. That April, terrorists bombed the finish line at the Boston Marathon. Three people were killed and 264 were injured in the attack. Afterward, the logos of the Red Sox and Yankees were displayed on a video board outside Yankee Stadium. Words on the video board said: "United We Stand." The Yankees held a moment of silence in honor of the victims and others affected. Yankees officials also played "Sweet Caroline" between innings. The famous Neil Diamond song is played in the middle of the eighth inning of every game at Fenway Park in Boston. Diamond later tweeted via social media: "Thank you NY Yankees for playing 'Sweet Caroline' for the people of Boston. You scored a home run in my heart."

//

WHAT IS IN A RIVALRY?

Police blame alcohol and drugs for some of these fights. But there are also deep emotions involved in rivalries. In many cases, people have been following a team for most of their lives. Their team might represent their hometown or way of life. Fans take great pride in their teams.

Scientific experiments have been conducted to examine the feelings of sports fans. In one of those experiments, three Princeton University psychological scientists studied a group of Yankees and Red Sox baseball fans. The fans were hooked up to a brain scanner while they watched videos of actual plays and games. The scanner measured the activity taking place in their brains. The fans were also asked specific feelings about a play. Did a stolen base make them angry? Did a bunt result in pleasure, or pain?

The results were published in an article by the Association for Psychological Science. The report stated: "The fans whose brains showed the greatest pleasure response to a rival player's failure—even if he was

A Boston Red Sox fan, *right*, and a New York Yankees fan, *left*, wear shirts jabbing at the other's team at a 2011 spring training game.

failing against the [Baltimore] Orioles rather than their own team—these fans were also the most aggressive fans."

The term for experiencing pleasure because of someone else's pain is called *schadenfreude*. The study found that fans experiencing this type of brain activity were more likely to take action during a game. Yankee fans might throw things at Red Sox fans, and Red Sox fans might do the same to Yankee fans.

HEALTHY RIVALRIES

Rivalries do not have to be violent, though. One of the fiercest rivalries in college football is between Army and Navy. These two service academies

Anna Mohr is a blogger on fansagainstviolence.com, a Web site devoted to fan safety at large stadiums across the United States. She is the sister of James Mohr, a New York Jets fan who was attacked in 2011. His attacker was sentenced to three years in prison. Mohr wrote:

> *I've often asked myself why violence on a baseball field, basketball court, or any other playing ground is treated any differently than the violence that occurs on the streets, amongst "regular" civilians. Why is [Philadelphia Phillies pitcher] Cole Hamels any different from the average Joe who picks up a hard object and throws it in the direct path of another human being? Why do we abhor the common assailant, yet feel a sense of allegiance to a member of our favored team, who, essentially, is guilty of the same offense?*

> Source: Mohr, Anna. "Could Intentional Violence on the Field Lead to More Violence in the Stands?" Fans Against Violence. *Fans Against Violence. 8 May 2012. Web. 8 Aug. 2013.*

Changing Minds

Do you agree with the writer? Should violence on a playing field be treated the same as violence on a street? Is it okay for sports fans to support the actions of a player on their favorite team, no matter what he or she does? Write an essay stating your opinion on this issue and do some research so that you are using a real-life example.

The annual Army-Navy football game is known for its tradition and mutual respect.

first played each other in 1890. They have played every year since 1930. Historically, Army and Navy were two of college football's powers. Now the programs are less competitive, but the game is still popular. It is played in a massive stadium on a neutral site and broadcast on national television each year.

The two teams badly want to beat each other. In 2012, Navy defeated Army for the eleventh year in a row. Afterward, television cameras

THE HEATED RIVALRIES

showed Army's quarterback crying. *USA Today* called it "one of the lasting memories from the 2012 college football season." However, the theme surrounding the game is tradition and respect. Students show up in official service uniforms to cheer on their teams. The president of the United States has been known to show up on occasion, too. Afterward the teams stand side by side on the field and sing each other's alma mater. The loser's song is played first.

"The rivalry between these two programs may be deeper than any other in the nation," Army veteran Levi Newman wrote, "but at the end of the day, away from the field of collegiate competition, they serve side-by-side for America."

Other rivals have shown similar unity. The University of Florida and the University of Georgia renew their fierce rivalry each fall on the football field. However, before the game the school's fans tailgate together in the "World's Largest Outdoor Cocktail Party." It is held at a neutral site in Jacksonville, Florida. In 1935, the governors of Iowa and Minnesota wagered a live pig in a friendly bet over the University of Iowa vs. University of Minnesota football game. The teams still battle each year for a pig named Floyd of Rosedale—only today the pig is a bronze trophy. Several other rivals play for similar trophies.

CHAPTER 3

A Clemson University fan climbs the goalpost after the ▶
Tigers' 2002 football victory over the rival University of
South Carolina.

STADIUM SECURITY: THE GAME PLAN FROM WITHIN

The annual Clemson University vs. University of South Carolina football game can produce a strong need for police officers. The game is a battle between rival schools in the same state. It features thousands of fans from both schools in one place. And both sides badly want to end the day with a win for their team.

When the game is played in Clemson, South Carolina, more than 81,000 fans attend at Memorial Stadium. South Carolina's home stadium, Williams-Brice Stadium in Columbia, also holds more than 80,000 people.

In November 2002, South Carolina traveled to Clemson for the annual game. It was the 110th time the two schools had played each other.

FATAL CELEBRATION

Dangerous celebrations are not limited to the massive crowds at major Division I sporting events. In 2005, tragedy struck at a Division III University of Minnesota-Morris football game. It was homecoming, and the team was playing its final game in an old stadium before moving to a new home. After a double-overtime win over Crown College, some of the approximately 1,000 fans charged the field to celebrate. They pulled down the goalposts. A falling goalpost hit 20-year-old student Richard Rose in the head. He died soon after due to head trauma.

And at the end of that meeting, Clemson won 27–20. The home fans wanted to celebrate. They rushed onto the field. And soon they made their way to the goalposts.

Homer Booth, a sheriff's deputy, was assigned to guard the goalposts at one end of the field. He was nearly trampled to death after he was knocked over.

"I couldn't breathe," he said. "I was pinned at the bottom, and I thought my life was going to be snuffed out."

Booth lost consciousness. He was transported to a hospital via ambulance. He suffered broken ribs and a broken collarbone. Booth was not the only one hurt. One fan had an arm broken in six places. Another lost three teeth. And yet another fan later needed knee surgery.

That same day, football players from the University of Cincinnati and the University of Hawaii threw punches instead of shaking hands after their game. The game was played in Honolulu, Hawaii. Hawaii fans threw water bottles and other things at Cincinnati players. Police used pepper spray to control the fans.

Beer cans pile up in a parking lot outside the ▲
Philadelphia Eagles' stadium before a 2009 NFL
game there.

"My wife was in the stands and I feared for her," said Bob Goin,
Cincinnati's athletics director.

LIMITING ALCOHOL

Thousands of athletes and fans attend sporting events each day and leave
without incident. But when incidents occur, sports teams and stadium
managers must be ready.

Stadium experts have cited alcohol as a major contributing factor
to fan violence and dangerous celebrations. That is one reason why
alcohol is banned at high school and many college sporting events. Most
professional sports teams sell alcohol in their stadiums. However, rules
usually require alcohol sales to end after a certain point in the game.

Some onlookers have called for an end to beer sales at stadiums. The issue arose after several fights between Oakland Raiders and San Francisco 49ers fans at a 2011 NFL game in San Francisco.

"Outlaw alcohol at the games," wrote Brad Stanhope of the *Daily Republic* in Fairfield-Suisun, California. "Don't sell it in the stadium, don't allow it in the parking lot. If you find someone smuggling it in, throw them out and prosecute them."

However, not everybody is in favor of limiting alcohol at sporting events. Many fans enjoy drinking during and before games. Teams also can make a lot of money by selling alcohol. And not all drinking takes place within the stadiums. Football fans are known for tailgating. Many fans show up at parking lots hours before a game. They grill food and play games, and some drink alcohol.

Gene Taylor was the sheriff of Anderson County, South Carolina, at the time of the 2002 Clemson-South Carolina game. He wanted Clemson to take steps to remove alcohol from parties in the parking lots. He threatened to stop assigning his police officers to games. Clemson officials told Taylor that his department's assistance was no longer needed. The school now hires private security instead.

The University of Missouri actually took a stand against rowdy tailgating. School officials cited numerous alcohol violations and fights as the reason for closing popular tailgating parking lot Reactor Field to fans in 2009. The school gave up potential revenue by closing the lot, which

had charged $15 per parked car. But senior associate athletics director
Whit Babcock said it needed to be done.

"It was a university decision but fully supported by the athletics
department and the MU Police Department," Babcock said. "It was
really just a behavioral issue down there. We were having fights, some
underage drinking."

FIELD SAFETY

Fans who storm a football field or a basketball court are usually
celebrating. The intent is not to injure one another. So it is not always
popular when schools and teams try to crack down on these celebrations.
But with the potential for danger, more and more schools are doing
just that.

Many schools have banned these types of celebrations. They hire security and police officers to keep fans off the field and away from the goalposts. At the University of Connecticut, police used pepper spray and police dogs to keep fans away from the goalposts. But even these measures often cannot always stop the hoard of rushing fans.

In 2004, the Southeastern Conference (SEC) began fining its member schools if they allowed fans to rush a field or court. The fines could range anywhere from $5,000 to $50,000. The University of Kentucky experienced this in 2010. Fans of the Wildcats rushed the football field that year after their team upset South Carolina. The SEC responded by fining Kentucky $25,000.

Many colleges now use collapsible goalposts. These can be taken down immediately after the game so fans cannot climb up and try to pull them down. The University of Colorado bought collapsible goalposts in the 1980s. But that did not stop Colorado students from rushing the field. However, Colorado assistant athletic director for facilities John Krueger said students no longer target the goalposts.

"Win or lose, we drop the posts," Krueger said. "Fans used to still go after the goalposts early on. They slowly figured out that they had little chance of getting to them prior to us getting them on the ground."

Some people are concerned that security at stadiums is too tough, however. In 2011, a security guard was caught on video tripping and pushing University of Minnesota students. The students had rushed the field to celebrate a football win over their rival, the University of Iowa. At a different college football game in 1999, security used tear gas to hold back fans.

TERRORISM THREATS

Public safety officers at sporting events are also preparing for potential terrorist threats. Terrorism refers to the use of violence or fear to intimidate people. Terrorists might attempt to use a sporting event to kill or injure innocent spectators. The bombings at the 2013 Boston Marathon raised the issue to a high level. Two terrorists set off bombs near the finish line to protest US government policies, killing three people and injuring 264.

Yet security budgets for major sporting events were growing rapidly before that. The Olympic Games draw the world's attention every two years. That makes the Games a target for terrorism. In 1972, terrorists kidnapped and eventually killed 11 Israeli athletes and officials. In 1996, a bomb killed one and injured more than 100 at a public concert during the Olympic Games in Atlanta. The terrorist attacks of September 11, 2001, increased awareness

TROUBLE IN THE BALLPARK

William Ligue Jr., then 34 years old, and his son, 15-year-old William III, ran onto the field at Comiskey Park in Chicago in September 2002. They attacked Tom Gamboa. Gamboa was a first-base coach for the Kansas City Royals. Security officers were unable to stop the assault at the beginning. The attack was so severe that Gamboa suffered permanent hearing loss. Ligue Jr. blamed drugs and alcohol. He said he was under the influence of cocaine, marijuana, and Valium. "To think I put my family and friends, Mr. Gamboa, his family and friends, and the city of Chicago [through that], I'm sorry," he told the *Daily Southtown* newspaper in October 2002.

▲ A woman shows off the clear plastic bag she brought to an NFL game after the league banned purses in 2013.

further. Security throughout the Olympic city, and especially the venues, is much stronger. Fans must go through security checkpoints just to enter the Olympic areas. In 2012, the security budget at the London Olympics was more than $800 million. Meanwhile, another more than $700 million was budgeted to cover army, security services, and police spending. The total budget for the Games was approximately $14.4 billion.

Outside of major events like the Olympic Games, just about every stadium has its own list of regulations for fans. There are rules for what fans can bring into a stadium and what they cannot. The NFL began scanning fans for metal objects in 2012. One year later, the NFL even banned most purses. That move proved to be unpopular. But bag searches at the University of Oklahoma football stadium might have prevented a tragedy in 2005.

Damon Zumwalt is the chairman and CEO of Contemporary Services Corporation (CSC). His company provides crowd management and stadium security services at sporting events. CSC staffers were doing bag checks at Oklahoma's Memorial Stadium gates in 2005 when an engineering student blew himself up just 200 yards (183 m) from the stadium. Zumwalt believes the student wanted to enter the stadium with a bomb inside a backpack. However, the student instead detonated the bomb while sitting on a nearby park bench. The Federal Bureau of Investigation (FBI) later concluded that it was not an act of terrorism.

Police, federal agents, and security guards searched Comerica Park after a bomb threat was made during a Detroit Tigers baseball game in 2012. The game went on and fans were not notified. No bomb was found. The stadium was never evacuated. However, some say fans were put at risk.

STADIUM NO-NOS

Teams in virtually every professional sports league have a list of regulations to govern the behavior of fans. The rules are in place to provide safety for fans at the event. They also help security officers and police keep the peace. The NFL's New England Patriots and Major League Soccer's Revolution have initiated a fan code of conduct. Among the prohibited items at their home field, Gillette Stadium in Foxboro, Massachusetts, are weapons, laser pointers, illegal drugs, food or beverages, noisemakers, and lacrosse balls. The Patriots went to a more restrictive list following the bombings at the 2013 Boston Marathon. Spectators also have to undergo a security screening before entering pro football or baseball stadiums.

In April 1993 in Hamburg, Germany, a fan ran onto the court and stabbed women's tennis star Monica Seles during a break in play. The incident changed Seles's life forever and, in a bigger sense, all of professional tennis. Seles later wrote about the incident:

> It's strange how the tiniest thing can have the most tremendous impact on your life. Doctors later told me that if I hadn't bent forward at that precise second, there was a good chance I would have been paralyzed. The cup had barely touched my lips when I felt a horrible pain in my back. Reflexively, my head whipped around toward where it hurt and I saw a man wearing a baseball cap and a vicious sneer across his face. His arms were raised above his head and his hands were clutching a long knife. He started to lunge at me again. I didn't understand what was happening: for a few seconds I sat frozen in my chair as two people tackled him to the ground. He had plunged the knife one and a half inches into my upper left back, millimeters away from my spine.

Source: Seles, Monica. *Getting a Grip: On My Body, My Mind, My Self. New York: Avery, 2009. Print.

What's the Big Idea

Read Monica Seles's description of the stabbing. One thing she could not understand was why it happened. Later, it became known that the German fan who stabbed her did not want Seles to be ranked the number-one player in the world. What do you think was going through Seles's mind as the incident happened? What could she have done?

"We don't make a decision to evacuate unless an actual [bombing] device is found," said Donald Johnson, an inspector in the Detroit Police Department's Homeland Security unit. "We don't panic. We go step by step. The thought was to find out what we actually had."

The bomb threat was another example of what stadium security officers must consider every day. Their job is to patrol the spectators at a sporting event in order to curb violence, but also to keep all of the fans safe.

STADIUM IMPROVEMENTS

Stepping in to help make stadiums safer is the National Center for Spectator Sports Safety and Security. The organization is more simply known as NCS4. It is based at the University of Southern Mississippi. It reviews hundreds of sports stadiums and arenas. NCS4 issues certification for the sports facilities that are the safest and have the best plans for fans.

NCS4 had reviewed 1,350 sports facilities by 2013. Only a third of those reviewed were taking necessary security measures, according to NCS4 director Lou Marciani. He said it is common to see different standards among different stadiums, and even from event to event.

NCS4 began its work in 2006. It has trained more than 900 universities and thousands of first responders. A first responder is a police officer, firefighter, or emergency medical technician. NCS4 has received $9.4 million in grants from the Office of Homeland Security and the US Department of Education.

Through 2013, a handful of universities were certified by the NCS4: University of Southern Mississippi, Mississippi State University, University of Mississippi, Texas A&M University, and Penn State University.

THE INTERNATIONAL SCENE

A popular movement had overthrown the Egyptian government in 2011. But people there were still unhappy with the new government in 2012. Activists accused the military and police of not intervening in times of trouble. Those feelings came out after a 2012 professional soccer game in Port Said, Egypt.

Fans of the home team, Al-Masry, rushed the soccer field. They had knives, clubs, and stones. They rushed against riot police. Many fans of the visiting team, Al-Ahly of Cairo, Egypt, were stuck. They clogged in an inside corridor while trying to escape the rival fans.

"Everyone was beating us. They were beating us from inside and outside [the stadium], with fireworks, stones, metal bars, and some knives, I swear," said one fan.

Sources differed on how many people were hurt. But it is believed that more than 70 people were killed and at least 200 people were injured in the incident after the game. Sharif Ikrami was a goalkeeper for Al-Ahly. He said the dead and wounded were brought into the team's locker room. It was enough for him to quit the game.

"There were people dying in front of us," he said. "It's over. We've all made a decision that we won't play soccer any more. How will we play soccer after 70 people died? We can't think about it."

MORE THAN A GAME

The culture surrounding sports can differ greatly in certain parts of the world. The reasons are many.

Simple geography can play a role. In the United States, major professional sports teams tend to be in cities hundreds of miles away from each other. In smaller countries, such as England, major cities often have two or more teams. In 2013–14, six of the 20 soccer teams in the English Premier League were from in or around London, England. Many of these

FC Barcelona fans wave pro-independence flags ▶
at the 2011 Copa del Rey final against rival
Real Madrid.

teams simply represent a neighborhood. And neighbors are natural rivals in just about any sport.

At the heart of many soccer conflicts, however, are politics and religion. Fans of some teams traditionally side with a specific religion, such as Celtic (Irish Catholic) and Rangers (Protestant) in Scotland. In Spain, FC Barcelona is located in an area known as Basque Country. Many Basque people wish to be independent from Spain. They view the soccer team as a major public representative for their larger struggle. These types of allegiances do not automatically lead to violence, but they often lead to more tension.

HOOLIGANISM

European soccer games have become safer, but soccer gangs and hooligans are still around. Often these hooligans stage fights and cause trouble outside the stadiums. Drugs and alcohol play a major role in hooligan culture. Soccer teams and leagues are taking steps to curb the violence, though. Pete Dearden is the football intelligence officer for Arsenal Football Club in London. He said security officers pay informants who might have information about where hooligans plan on meeting.

HOOLIGAN CULTURE

Another issue with European soccer is the hooligan culture. Hooligans are people who purposely create violence at sporting events. They are most affiliated with soccer. Often these hooligans belong to gangs of hard-core supporters for certain teams. They attend home games and also many away games. Often they drink excessively beforehand. And often they get into fights with other fans or cause trouble in the stadiums or in the surrounding streets and pubs.

English soccer fans developed a reputation for hooliganism in the 1970s and 1980s. At the 1985 European Cup final, Liverpool fans charged an opposing fan group, killing 39 people. For a period, English fans were banned from traveling to games in other countries. They still sometimes went, though, and caused trouble outside the stadiums.

English soccer officials have taken great measures to limit hooliganism. Stadiums are now safer. Security at the games is better prepared. However, hard-core fan groups still exist in England and many other countries. One of the most notorious fan groups supports the team Lazio in Italy.

Some Lazio fans are neo-Nazis. They hold banners with Nazi messages at games. They taunt and boo black and Jewish players. In 2012, Lazio fans staged an

THE HILLSBOROUGH DISASTER

For many years, international soccer stadiums had sections called terraces. These areas had large steps for fans to stand but did not include seats. Sometimes they included barriers along the edges to physically separate opposing fan groups. Terraces were notorious havens for violence, especially in England. The end of terraces began thanks to a terrible accident. In 1989, fans crowded into Hillsborough Stadium in Sheffield, England, for a game between Liverpool and Nottingham Forest. The terrace at Hillsborough was meant for approximately 1,500 fans, but around 3,000 were allowed in. Fans tried to escape, but the barriers around the section made that difficult. As a result, hundreds of fans were crushed and 96 people died. A report estimated that nearly half of those deaths might have been avoided. However, police and stadium officials took a long time to react, assuming fans were just being rowdy. The disaster resulted in safer stadiums being built across England.

Fans of the Italian team Lazio display a flag with ▶
the Nazi swastika symbol during a 2005 game
against rival Roma.

organized attack against visiting fans of Tottenham Hotspur, an English team with Jewish roots.

Official and independent soccer organizations are working to reduce racism and violence at games. University of Michigan professor Andrei S. Markovits authored a research article for the *Harvard International Review* in 2011. He examined the differences between violence at sports events in other countries and the isolated cases of violence in the United States.

"Soccer [stadiums] have become the last bastion in contemporary Europe in which the worst kind of racist, sexist, anti-Semitic . . . language and behavior have not only been tolerated, but actually extolled." Meanwhile, he wrote that while discrimination and racism remain an issue in the United States, "overt racism has for all intents and purposes been banned from contemporary US sports."

INTERNATIONAL DIFFERENCES

Andrei S. Markovits is a professor of comparative politics and German studies at the University of Michigan. He wrote about the differences between the United States and other countries in the *Harvard International Review* in 2011. "In perhaps the greatest contrast to its European counterparts, these US instances of fan violence have not been accompanied by racial hatred, overt racism, or anti-Semitism," he wrote. "Jeering the New York Yankees and deriding the Michigan Wolverines with vulgar language might not be pretty, but it constitutes a different category than spewing hatred and venom against Jews, blacks, and other nonwhite minorities as has remained commonplace in Europe's stadiums since the 1970s."

CHAPTER 5

A fight breaks out in the stands during the Alabama state basketball tournament in 2009. ▶

SAFETY AT ALL LEVELS

The roles change dramatically for adults and kids at youth sports events. Adults at professional sporting events are often attending as fans. But at a youth sporting event, an adult might be a coach, team manager, referee, or umpire. Instead of a child being a fan, he or she is likely to be a player in the game.

In the United States, approximately 44 million kids between the ages of 6 and 18 play sports. Many of those kids play in community-based sports leagues, according to the National Council of Youth Sports (NCYS). Those leagues require 3 million adults who are serving as coaches or in other positions. Many of those adults are parents.

Adults are supposed to serve as role models and protectors for youth athletes. The adults do not always do a good job. A fight at a youth football game in Arizona in 2012 included parents, coaches, and children. The incident started when a parent yelled his disagreement at the calls made by a referee. The referee asked for the parent to leave, but the parent refused. A fight broke out and ended with kids getting hurt and one being transported to a hospital by ambulance. Five players and three coaches were suspended by Northern AZ Youth Football.

In California in 2012, police in riot gear were called to a youth football game to break up a fight among parents. In Georgia in 2013, a team's head coach and a player's mom were jailed following a battle at a youth baseball game. The incident began with name-calling.

In one extreme example, a father in California ran onto the field during a youth football game to tackle a member of the opposing team. In another, a parent of a 10-year-old ice hockey player beat the team's coach to death.

POWDER-PUFF FOOTBALL

Fights and aggressive behavior are not limited to men's sports. Powder-puff football is a tradition at many high schools. These games usually involve girls playing flag football against girls from a different class. Sometimes a boys' football player will coach them. The games are often held around homecoming. The intent is for the games to be a fun activity for all of the students. However, these games have sometimes turned violent. That has caused some schools to cancel them. One such school was Century High School in North Dakota. "It stopped because it turned quickly from a fun, jovial type football game into a game where it was girls wanting to take a shot at another girl, and not really playing the game," principal Steve Madler said. "So it's more about taking somebody out than actually just going out and playing the game."

Examples like these are extreme. Experts believe the high-profile examples make the problem look worse than it is. However, even less serious examples of misbehaving parents can be problematic. Studies have shown that positive parental support can have a major impact on youth athletes. The challenge is getting all parents to buy in.

BETTER BEHAVIOR

Lindsey C. Blom, EdD, and Dan Drane, PhD, work at the School of Human Performance and Recreation at the University of Southern Mississippi. They wrote in an article published online by Athletic Insight that "positive parent support is related to positive sport experiences for children."

MISCONDUCT NUMBERS

A 2005 survey of youth sports issues highlighted the problems of parental interference. Doug Abrams, a law professor at the University of Missouri, and youth sports advocate Bob Bigelow did the survey. Of the nearly 100 responses, 71 percent cited parent misconduct as the worst problem in youth sports. Fifty-one percent of the respondents also mentioned coaching misconduct as a major problem. Many also said there was too much emphasis placed on winning.

///////////////////////

A study was done of 110 parents attending their kids' youth sports events. An analysis showed that 31 percent of parents' comments were reinforcing in nature. Meanwhile, 28 percent were corrective.

A panel of youth sports experts rated the behavior and involvement of parents as unacceptable in the 2005 Youth Sports National Report Card. A movement to fix that unacceptable behavior is underway. Many youth sports teams and leagues now require parents and players to sign a code of conduct. The document becomes a social contract. Human Kinetics Inc. has developed a series of classes and educational products for coaches. The NCYS has produced a number of videos targeted for parents and coaches. The coaching instruction stresses safety and player development while discouraging the win-at-all-cost philosophy. The parent videos address health, safety, and character and skill development, as well as the idea of sports parenting.

WATCHING OUT FOR REFS

Conflict between coaches or athletes and game officials is not new. Officials have long been blamed for bad calls or calls that fans disagree

RICARDO PORTILLO

Referee
Liga Continental
de Futbol

⊻ MITSUBISHI ELECTRIC

Seattle Sounders fans observe a moment of ▲
silence for youth soccer referee Ricardo Portillo
in May 2013.

with. However, the recent intensity with which officials are being attacked has some concerned.

In New Jersey, a parent slapped a 17-year-old Little League Baseball umpire. Jayme Ream was the referee at a youth football game in 2011 in Sarasota, Florida. One team disagreed with one of Ream's calls. Coaches, parents, and a teenage player physically assaulted Ream.

Ream suffered a fractured shoulder. Three coaches and a 14-year-old player faced felony charges. Attacking a referee in Florida is a felony. Ream filed suit against the Sarasota County School District because the game was played on one of its athletic fields.

An assault on a referee can be deadly. Ricardo Portillo was refereeing a youth soccer game in 2013 in Utah. A 17-year-old player did not like one of

Portillo's calls. So the teen punched Portillo in the face. The punch caused brain swelling. Portillo died soon after. In 2012, another soccer official died following an assault by a group of players in the Netherlands.

Portillo was the second sports official in the United States to die from an assault, according to the National Association of Sports Officials (NASO). But NASO president Barry Mano added that some assaults likely go unreported.

Fears of verbal or physical abuse have played a role in referee shortages across the United States. A survey of 60 high school athletic associations showed that many states are losing officials. Most states license officials on an annual basis. According to a NASO survey, the biggest reason for officials not returning is the lack of sportsmanship.

Doug Harvey is a longtime umpire in MLB. He recognizes the dangers umpires face at the youth sports level. "Violence is clearly a reflection of society," he said. "You have drivers shooting at each other, then you're gonna have moms and pops attacking Little League umpires. Many people evidently feel they can solve problems through physical retaliation."

Community officials are trying to make changes to protect referees. In Buffalo Grove, Illinois, signs were installed at parks around town in an attempt to improve adult behavior during youth athletic events. The idea was the brainchild of Mike Terson. He is a park district official who had seen similar signs in other communities. Among the messages on the signs: "No one shouts at you in front of other people when you make a mistake, so please don't yell at them. We do not have video replay; so, we will go with their calls."

Some states have gone even further, passing legislation to protect officials. California's legislation is one of the stiffest. An assault against a sports official there can result in a $2,000 fine and a one-year prison sentence. An assault against an ordinary citizen carries penalties half as stiff.

MAKING EVENTS SAFER

Approximately 11 million people compete in high school sports. An estimated 336 million fans attend high school basketball and football games each year. That has caught the attention of the NCS4. In 2013, NCS4 began a pilot program at three Mississippi high schools to address security needs. NCS4 officials hope to turn it into a national program.

The high school program at NCS4 picked up momentum after the December 2012 school shootings at an elementary school in Newtown, Connecticut. Lou Marciano is the executive director for

///////////////////////////////

SPORTSMANSHIP

Sportsmanship is mentioned in virtually every league code of conduct or list of regulations. Darrell Erickson is a sales manager and volunteer youth sports coach. He says there is no middle ground. There is good sportsmanship and bad sportsmanship. In his book, *Molding Young Athletes*, Erickson says it is important for parents and coaches to show good sportsmanship. He wrote: "Our good behaviors should also be extended to the umpires, referees, and judges. Remind every player they are representing their school, community, or organization."

///////////////////////////////////////

Officials are working to ensure that sports ▶
stadiums can be a place for positive,
safe entertainment.

NCS4. He participated in a session on school safety at the White House in Washington DC. Marciano said the number of people coming onto campus after school for sporting events requires different strategies than security during in-school hours. Schools might have emergency plans in place during school hours but not necessarily for after-school events, Marciano said. NCS4 is working with the National Federation of State High School Associations (NFHS) and National Interscholastic Athletic Administrators Association (NIAAA) to develop a "standardized sports risk-management practices plan for high school events," Marciano said.

Removing all violence from sports might be impossible. But changes on every level, from new government laws to new attitudes from parents, are helping make sports more enjoyable for all involved: athletes, referees, coaches, and fans.

DISCUSSION QUESTIONS

Another View

The book begins with a detailed description of a brawl between the Indiana Pacers and the Detroit Pistons that went into the stands during an NBA game. Some blamed the fans. Some blamed the players. Some blamed the Pistons for not having enough security at the game. Who do you think is to blame for the brawl? And what could have been done to prevent the fight in the stands?

Why Do I Care?

Parents and players are now being required to sign codes of conduct at many schools and youth sports leagues. Is this something that you or your parents have already done? Write a 200-word essay describing how this affects you. Do you think this is a good idea? And do the parents and players follow the code of conduct?

Tell the Tale

The second chapter of this book discusses many of the heated college and professional sports rivalries that exist in the United States. Come up with a list of five sports rivalries that you know about. It can include high school rivalries or club sports rivalries. What do all of the rivalries have in common with each other?

assault

A physical or verbal attack.

code of conduct

A document, or social contract, that is signed by parents and sometimes players in the interest of good sportsmanship.

commissioner

The chief executive of a sports league.

felony

A serious crime.

pundit

A person who gives opinions, often in the mass media. In many cases, a pundit may be a writer or a broadcaster.

riot

A large-scale display of civil disorder.

rival

An opponent that brings out great emotion in a team and its fans.

tailgate

A party held in a stadium parking lot prior to a game.

FOR MORE INFORMATION

SELECTED BIBLIOGRAPHY

Erickson, Darrell. *Molding Young Athletes*. Oregon, WI: Purington Press, 2004. Print.

Garlett, Kyle, and Patrick O'Neal. *The Worst Call Ever!* New York: HarperCollins Publishing, 2007. Print.

Goodman, Gary S. *101 Things Parents Should Know Before Volunteering to Coach Their Kids' Sports Teams*. Lincolnwood, IL: Contemporary Books, 2000. Print.

Seles, Monica. *Getting a Grip: On My Body, My Mind, My Self*. New York: Avery, 2009. Print.

FURTHER READINGS

Araton, Harvey. *Crashing the Borders*. New York: Free Press, 2005. Print.

Brimson, Dougie. *March of the Hooligans: Soccer's Bloody Fraternity*. New York: Virgin Books, 2007. Print.

Martens, Rainer. *Joy and Sadness in Children's Sports*. Champaign, IL: Human Kinetics, 1978. Print.

WEB SITES

To learn more about violence in sports, visit ABDO Publishing Company online at **www.abdopublishing.com**. Web sites about violence in sports are featured on our Book Links page. These links are routinely monitored and updated to provide the most current information available.

PLACES TO VISIT

National Baseball Hall of Fame and Museum
25 Main Street
Cooperstown, NY 13326
888-HALL-OF-FAME
www.baseballhall.org
The Baseball Hall of Fame is open to the public daily except for Thanksgiving, Christmas, and New Year's Day. The Hall of Fame includes a history of baseball, its rivalries, and a large number of memorabilia and artifacts.

Newport Sports Museum
100 Newport Center Drive #100
Newport Beach, CA 92660
949-721-9333
www.newportsportsmuseum.org
This museum aims to promote healthy lifestyles through its memorabilia and partnerships with famous athletes. In addition, the museum has free programs meant to help instill confidence in children and teens.

INDEX

ABOUT THE AUTHOR

Paul D. Bowker is a freelance writer and author based in Chesterton, Indiana. He has authored four other books on MLB, the NBA, and women's lacrosse. He is also a high school soccer official licensed in three states. He is national past president of Associated Press Sports Editors, and has won several national and state writing awards. He lives with his wife and daughter.